THE ATM

FASTLANE

THE ATM

FASTLANE

HOW TO QUIT YOUR JOB BY BUILDING YOUR OWN ATM EMPIRE

BY:

SEAN FINE & RYAN TIMBERG

TABLE OF CONTENTS

WHO IS ACME ATM?

Before we begin explaining the step-by-step model for launching and growing your own ATM business, let us explain who we are. Acme is an ATM Placement and Processing company based in South Florida. Our network stretches across America, where we've spent years building our expertise and experience.

Our business has two primary focuses: first, we work hand in hand with entrepreneurs who are either starting from scratch or looking to grow their current ATM portfolio. By working with Acme, entrepreneurs benefit from our strategic guidance and expertise in finding profitable locations, negotiating and closing deals, portfolio management, marketing, and more. We also provide all ATMs and supplies, installations, programming, and cash loading services, with the goal of streamlining and simplifying the process of running an ATM business. Second, Acme provides Full Placement and Processing services to a variety of businesses looking to earn extra passive income while offering their customers access to cash, including hotels, nightclubs, bars, markets, and gas stations.

Ultimately, this book is aimed at Acme's first focus, entrepreneurs. In the following chapters, we share the breadth of knowledge and experience we've amassed over the years to launch and grow an ATM business. We've outlined our proven formula in an easy-to-follow checklist format. Combine the tools and knowledge presented in this book with dedication and a little hard work, and soon enough, you will be earning a stable side income and on track to replace your job income.

Ready to get started? Keep reading and learn how to start an ATM business today.

You can learn more about us at
ATMResidualincome.com.

PREFACE

It's 6:00am, Monday morning. I like to wake up before the sun wakes me up. I jump up on my doorframe pull-up bar for ten energizing repetitions. I then head to the kitchen to make my bulletproof coffee concoction. I slink into my recliner to practice 10 minutes of mindfulness meditation. Once my mind is clear and centered and my body vitalized, I open my iPhone to access my online banking app. I navigate to the morning's deposits and begin to grin. As a result of Fridays, Saturdays, and Sunday's withdrawal transactions, more than $1,000 was deposited into our business account as profit from a weekend of arduous intensive labor.

My witty sarcasm may have eluded you. To be frank, when I say arduous intensive labor, I mean I took a mini-honeymoon with my beautiful wife to Tulum, Mexico. We relaxed on white sandy beaches, ate at world-class restaurants, toured ancient Mayan ruins, enjoyed Mayan clay massages, and snorkeled in cavernous freshwater sinkholes formed millions of years ago along the Yucatán peninsula called cenotes.

I tell you this story because it is a vignette of the quintessential "make money while you sleep" lifestyle that has become pervasive throughout the modern American workforce. Making money while you sleep is, ironically, merely a dream for most workers. The idea of trading time for money is entrenched in us. The output of 1 hour of work in exchange for an hourly wage. You can't earn unless you're working.

In 2007, Tim Ferriss, in his brilliant book the 4-Hour Workweek, offered the workforce a new life/work paradigm, essentially flipping the concept of trading time for dollars on its head. Ferriss suggests beginning with a lifestyle outcome, an ideal lifestyle setup for you, and working backward to fill in the gaps. For example, if your outcome is to live and travel through Asia for a year, then find or create a job that allows for this financially and practically. Alternatively, if your outcome is to simply spend more time with your family at home rather than with colleagues at the office, Ferriss offers strategies and tactics to help influence your boss to allow you to work more remotely. Ultimately, Ferriss is demonstrating a better way to make money and enjoy your life outside of the construct of the classic 9 to 5 paradigm.

I read the 4-Hour Workweek in 2011 while working for a boutique law firm in Miami Shores, Florida, as a new lawyer practicing commercial litigation. The legal profession is glorified on television through shows such as Law & Order and most recently Suits. Hollywoodization of the legal profession makes it appear glamorous and thrilling. Well, I hate to burst your bubble, as mine was certainly burst, it's not. I had two bosses and continuous deadlines constantly breathing down my neck. My office was a jungle of paperwork. My fingertips were raw from drafting document after document. People think novelists write a lot, but I can attest any lawyer writes more words in their lifetime comparatively. Plainly, the job was not glitzy, or fulfilling, for that matter. I dreaded each and every day. If I had less than ten emails waiting for me in my inbox on a Sunday morning, it was a pleasant Sunday. I knew I had to make a change. Not merely a change of profession, but a massive shift in my way of thinking about the design of my life.

Fast forward to July 2013, Chicago, Illinois. On stage, performance and life coach Tony Robbins is bouncing, dancing, and clapping about, sweat flying off his leathery cheeks showering the first three rows of attendees. I am absorbing these antics ten rows back representing my city proudly sporting my teal Miami Dolphins T-shirt when my gaze catches a man wearing the exact same shirt nearby. My (in the moment) explanation is, of course, fate, so I made my way over to him to introduce myself. His name was Mike, and he owned and operated an ATM company in South Florida. To satisfy my curiosity, he explained the business model and how he made money, and I was instantly hooked. After the event, we kept in touch, and a month later, I was working with him at his company. Over the next year, I would learn as much as I could from a pro operating over 1500 locations nationwide.

In late 2014, due to unfortunate circumstances regarding Mike's health, I was forced to move on from the company. Immediately after I left, I founded Acme ATM with my business partner Ryan Timberg, the co-author of this book. I met and became close with Ryan while working at Mike's company. Ryan's background is in IT and computers, and he happens to be a wizard with ATMs. Hence, Ryan's position as Acme's Chief Technology Officer. Since Ryan and I joined forces, we've grown Acme to over 500 ATM locations, and we're not stopping there.

Along our journey from 0 to 500 locations, we've learned tricks of the trade and discovered which strategies work, and which don't. We've memorialized our blueprint in the following chapters of this book. Anyone with an entrepreneurial mindset can utilize this book as a guide to take a similar path and build a business for themselves. Whether you are a serial entrepreneur, part-time, or full-time employee looking to replace or supplement your income, this book will show you a path to achieving that outcome.

I've come to realize that most people don't start a project or make a change in their lives due to fear. However, that specific fear is difficult to pinpoint. It could be any of fear of failure, fear of change, fear of shaking things up, fear of disappointing people, and most notably, fear of success. It's important to focus on the reasons *why* you must take the actions you are contemplating taking. What will creating a passive income streams do for your life? Who will it help you impact? How will it help you spend your time? Who are you hurting in the long run if you don't take action now? Yourself? Your family?

Knowing your *why* will incentivize you to learn the *how*. The *how* is the simple part. That's what this book is for.

> **"WHAT WE FEAR DOING MOST IS USUALLY WHAT WE MOST NEED TO DO."**
>
> **—TIMOTHY FERRISS, THE 4 HOUR WORKWEEK**

ATM BUSINESS OVERVIEW

CHAPTER 1

HOW TO MAKE MONEY WITH ATMS

Have you ever started pumping gas at a gas station and filled the time by pulling out cash because it's useful in emergencies, or eaten dinner at a restaurant that doesn't accept credit cards, or wanted to leave a tip for your bartender? Maybe, you've had a negative experience with card theft or identity theft, and out of an abundance of caution, you prefer to only pay with cash. Perhaps you've found yourself in a situation where you desire purchase privacy or anonymity. Or, simply, you're partial to paying for everyday items in cash because it's easier to budget, not pile up debt, and keep track of expenditures.

So, you head to the nearest ATM and find that it charges a $3 fee to take out cash. Have you ever wondered who earns that $3 fee? Well, you might be surprised to find out that it's not the banks!

In fact, the person making that money is usually an individual just like you – someone who was interested in making a second income, or maybe someone who wanted to start his/her own business and leave the world of offices and 9-to-5 schedules behind. That person now makes an income based on this very simple premise:

An ATM filled with vault cash is placed in a high-traffic area where people have a need for cash. Whenever cash is withdrawn from that ATM, the owner collects a fee. At the end of the month, the ATM owner pays the location owner a portion of the fee as part of the agreement to house the ATM.

That's it! You might be thinking it sounds too simple and is likely one of those "too good to be true" business models. However, sometimes, simple is what works the best, and owning ATMs is a perfect example.

Beyond this basic setup, there are only a few other things that really must be considered or managed. The first is monitoring your machine with the use of software. You can track how much cash is in each machine in real-time so that you never have to guess when cash in a machine needs to be replenished. This allows you to manage your ATMs remotely and in minimal time.

The second thing that you need to know is how you are going to be compensated. When a customer withdraws $100 from your ATM for a $3 fee, $100 from the customer's bank and the $3 fee are deposited into your account the next day. No more waiting for payday to fill up your car or having to tighten your belt at the end of the month; you'll have new income every single day that your machine is used.

Here's an example to help you see exactly how simple and profitable this business can be: let's say that you purchase one ATM (roughly $2,500) and set it up in the perfect location; a popular bar downtown, a location with strong demand for cash and heavy foot traffic. You fill it with $2,000 cash, enough to last approximately one week. You charge $3 per transaction to withdraw cash and are averaging 200 transactions a month. This results in $600 revenue each month.

You pay a $1 commission for each of the 200 transactions to the location owner. Accordingly, after subtracting the $200 commission payment from the $600 revenue, your result is a $400 profit.

In one month, you earned $400 of extra income. Since you filled the ATM with enough cash requiring only one refill visit per week to the machine, that $400 of income was the result of almost no work on your part whatsoever. With your handy software monitoring everything, you didn't waste time traveling to the machine to check the cash level. The location owner kept the ATM area safe, clean, and accessible to customers. And, the best part, your income was deposited directly into your bank account daily.

This example shows just how easy it can be to start earning a side income with ATMs, but this business isn't limited to a bit of extra cash or merely a side hustle. Let's take a look at how you can replace your current income and 9-5 office lifestyle with ATMs.

CHAPTER 2

HOW TO USE ATMS TO ACHIEVE INDEPENDENCE

In the example from Chapter 1, you saw how realistic it is to earn an extra income every month. In our example, it was $400, but with five ATMs, it would have been $2,000. Further, your daily time investment is disproportionately low compared to the amount of added monthly income. If you want to save for vacations or large purchases, make extra payments on your house or car every month, or simply bolster your bank account and build an emergency fund, even a single ATM can drastically help achieve these goals.

At this point, you're either satisfied with your extra $400 of income each month, or you have a vision of replicating the process and effort exerted to acquire and manage your sole location. Let me add a note of caution, flourishing ATM locations are not ubiquitous. $400 of ATM profit simply doesn't exist on every street corner. To maximize profit potential, you need to be strategic and target specific types of locations identified later in the book. For example, because gas stations, hotels, and nightclubs are highly profitable locations, there will be fierce competition to earn their ATM accounts. On the other hand, salons, barbershops, and car washes will earn you less profit, but the barrier to entry is lower.

As a side note, you might be wondering why a location doesn't simply buy and operate their own ATM cutting out the middleman. The main reason is that owning and operating an ATM is not the primary business of the location. A hotel or restaurant doesn't want to dedicate time, money, and energy managing an ATM. Their business is hospitality, not ATMs. ATMs, similar to vending machines, are rarely owned by the location. Even in the rare instance where a location would like to own an ATM and manage it themselves, they will still need you to process their machine. This setup will be further explained in a later chapter.

Taking our example from Chapter 1 a step further, what if you decide you want more than merely a side income? What if you want to quit your boring desk job and start finally living life on your own terms? What if you determine you have the ability to become your own boss with an ATM business by replicating your success from Chapter 1 over and over? In the following example, we'll use the same numbers from

Chapter 1, but we'll do it on a scale five times larger than before.

After doing your homework, you identify four more spots around town with all the traits of a profitable location: a lack of nearby banks, a prevalence of businesses where cash is expected, and heavy foot traffic patterns. You approach the owners and hustle to earn their business. The result is you have five total locations earning $400 profit each month. You have now successfully created a side business earning $2,000 in monthly profit, an extra $24,000 annually. This is a significant amount of money.

Once you have five machines and understand the process, how difficult would it be to install ten? Soon enough, your additional $2,000 per month income becomes $4,000. And with your software monitoring each machine, it's easy to keep them all filled and operational around the clock.

Simply by scaling up from a single machine to five, 10, or more, you could go from supplementing your income to completely replacing it. As your own boss, you choose when you work, how often you work, and what you work on. You are in charge of the way you run your business. You choose whether to keep your business small and local or to expand your footprint across nearby cities and towns. You may grow so large that you're able to contract out your loading and machine servicing, freeing up even more of your time.

All this is completely reasonable and possible, thanks to the simple model that the ATM business provides. To understand the business completely and why it's extremely popular, let's take a look at the benefits.

CHAPTER 3

THE BENEFITS OF OWNING AN ATM BUSINESS

There are no limitations on who can earn money with ATMs. Business owners, landlords, management companies, and individual entrepreneurs are just a few examples of who might choose to start earning a passive income from ATMs.

Making money with ATMs is attractive because it's a straightforward business to learn, understand, implement, and manage. Anyone can begin by seeking out a profitable long-term location, installing an ATM, and putting cash in it for withdrawal. If a machine isn't making as much income as you anticipated, simply move it to a new location.

In Chapter 2, we touched briefly on the strategy of using ATMs to achieve independence. Now let's take an in-depth look at *why* starting an ATM business is one of the best life and career decisions you'll ever make.

1. You become your own boss with the ability to create your own schedule.

Ultimately, time is our most valuable resource. Once it's spent, it cannot be earned back. Most people feel trapped and detest how much time they're obligated to spend clocked in at their 9-5 job. This is time spent on someone else's dreams.

Do you ever wish you could steal your time back? What if you could work four fruitful days per week manifesting your own dreams and have the remainder of the week to spend with your family or pursue interests? What if you had the flexibility to go for a run during the day, or pick up the kids from school, take a guitar lesson, or spend a three-day weekend on the coast? This type of schedule flexibility isn't possible for employees, but if you own your business, you have complete control over your schedule and, ultimately, your life.

Savvy business owners know putting in hard focused work is necessary. The question is, just how much do you need to put in to achieve your desired outcome? After doing the research to find the best locations and having your machines installed, the only regular task you'll need to perform is loading the machines with cash. In our experience, a 10-machine business requires, at most, two workdays of loading per week and can generate thousands of dollars per month.

2. **You are in complete control of your own success. You also define it.**

As an ATM business owner, you alone are in charge of how successful you are. You aren't beholden to working toward other organizations' desired goals, utilizing their practices, or adhering to metrics chosen by others to define your success. Instead, you get to choose what goal to work toward, which carrot dangling from the end of the stick to chase. You get to decide the how and the when and the where. And most importantly, you get to hold yourself accountable. The results are a direct reflection of your effort.

If you define success as $10,000 per month in income, you can calculate exactly how many locations you need to acquire. Using our $400 per month profit example, to earn $10,000 per month, you'll need 25 locations. Under your own definition of success, you will be successful in just over two years if you install one ATM per month for the next 25 months.

3. An ATM business is easy to monitor and manage.

To monitor and manage your machines, you will use free web-based proprietary software given to you by your processing company. This software allows you to see exactly how much cash is in the machine at any given time. You never have to guess or randomly stop by to check on a machine. You'll receive a text message and/or email alert when a cash balance falls below a predetermined amount allowing you to easily schedule your work ahead of time. This same software notifies you if a machine goes offline for any reason, so you can attend to it as soon as possible.

Further, to pay your locations, you can spend one day per month writing and mailing checks. A more preferred method may be to pay your locations automatically through direct deposit. This puts commission payments on complete autopilot.

4. Typically, ATM owners do not have employees.

Interviewing, hiring, training, managing, paying, and trusting employees are time-consuming and challenging tasks. Fortunately, the structure of an ATM business is such that a sole owner can run it efficiently and effectively without employees. You can easily contract out your installations, machine servicing, and even your cash loading. As you expand, you may decide to hire an office manager or sales agent, but for the most part, ATM businesses can be run entirely by yourself. In effect, the ATMs are your employees.

5. **ATM business bookkeeping and accounting are simple.**

You don't need to be a tax professional to understand the cash flow and accounting behind an ATM business. The revenue from machines is reliably deposited into your bank account each day based on the previous day's revenue.

Your responsibilities are summed up as follows: paying location owners their monthly or quarterly commission from your account, tracking income and expenses, and preparing and filing taxes. You have the option to prepare them yourself or hire a tax professional. Generally, there is no need to pay overheads, such as for office space or payroll, as you can work from home and have no employees.

6. **Risk decreases the more locations you have.**

The more machines you have, the smaller the business risk becomes because the risk is distributed evenly across all locations.

For example, if you have 10 locations, and you lose one for any reason, temporarily or permanently, you still have 90% of your machines working and earning profits. When you either fix or find a new location for that 10th machine, you'll be quickly back to firing on all cylinders.

LAUNCHING AND GROWING AN ATM BUSINESS – A → Z

CHAPTER 4

STARTUP COSTS

Thus far, we've talked about all the ways that owning an ATM business can be beneficial and how easy it is to start and manage. After understanding the general principles, the first question people ask is, what are the startup costs? As with nearly all businesses, some capital is required upon startup.

Under the structure we've discussed thus far, your goal is to place your own ATM inside a business from which customers of that business can withdraw cash. This structure is called a Placement Deal. You buy a machine, install it in a location, and put your own cash for people to withdraw. You have 100% ownership of the machine. In our experience, the capital requirements to launch your first Placement Deal is $4,000 - $6,000. Here is the breakdown:

ATM machine: On average, $2,500.

Cash for customers to withdraw: $1,500. However, this amount varies based on the number of transactions and how often you desire to refill the machine. If the machine goes through $1,500 a week, you have to refill once per week. If it goes through $3,000 per week, you'll need to refill the machine twice per week.

Installation tools: Tools are a one-time cost that can vary depending on where you buy them. Lowe's and the Home Depot typically have the lowest prices. However, if you contract with a company such as Acme for your installations, you won't need tools at all.

Wireless box: If the location you've chosen does not have a phone line or local internet connection, plan on spending roughly $20 per month for a wireless box that uses Verizon or AT&T cellular connection. Wireless boxes enable the ATM to connect to the networks and banks to process transactions.

All these expenses add up to between $4,000 and $6,000 in expected startup costs.

With that said, there is an alternative deal structure where startup costs are $0. Up to this point, we've only discussed Placement Deals, but there's another deal structure to learn to add to your arsenal.

A Processing Deal, albeit used infrequently, is appropriate when a location wants to own and manage their own ATM. You sell them an ATM, install it, and connect their machine to your processing network. This model requires $0 to start because you are not purchasing an ATM or using your cash. You make money from selling the ATM for more than you can purchase it for and from ongoing processing fees on each transaction.

CHAPTER 5

STEP 1 - FORMING A COMPANY

The first step to getting started in the ATM business is deciding what business entity you will operate.

There are several options from which to choose, each having advantages and disadvantages. The most common entities are a sole proprietorship, an LLC, and a corporation. Here is a brief description, costs, and benefits of each to help you select the best option based on your needs.

Sole Proprietorship

A sole proprietorship is the easiest form of doing business. Simply begin selling your product or service because there are no formalities required or documents to file with the state. You don't need a tax ID, nor do you need a business bank account.

Although it's easy to get started, there are important disadvantages to this structure. First, sole proprietors are subject to a self-employment tax on ordinary net income earned by the business. Second, your assets are personally exposed, leaving you personally responsible for any liabilities of the business, debt and lawsuits included. In addition, your personal credit is also your business credit. In contrast, corporations and LLCs build credit from scratch. Building corporate credit takes time and is a major asset when built properly. Further, your image as a company will be yourself rather than a corporate name unless you file to operate under a DBA (doing business as). This portrays a lack of legitimacy to prospective customers if you're just beginning in the ATM field.

LLC or S Corporation

A smarter strategy is to form an LLC or an S corporation, both of which shelter you from personal responsibility for business liabilities and may save you money in taxes. Your LLC or S corp will open a business bank account to keep business and personal funds separate. Generally, LLCs do not offer the same self-employment tax savings as S corps do, but you can elect an LLC to be taxed as if it were an S corp. Lastly, operating as an entity makes you appear more legitimate and trustworthy to potential clients.

Legal Disclaimer: We recommend consulting with a business-centric certified accounting professional and attorney for advice and to assist you with creating an entity tailored to your needs. We do not offer legal advice.

For a more detailed description and explanation on business structures and tax information, we recommend reading Start Your Own Corporation by Garrett Sutton, Esq. and The Tax & Legal Playbook: Game-Changing Solutions for Your Small-Business Questions by Mark J Kohler, CPA, Esq.

Naming and Branding

If you do decide that starting a company is the best way to operate your ATM business, you need to name and brand it. Think of your brand as your promise to your customers – what they can expect from you in every interaction. For example, as a company that deals with people's money, you'll likely want to portray a brand of trustworthiness, honesty, and integrity.

The first and most important part of branding is the name. Your name should embody a promise to your customers, and it should sound professional. If you've chosen Abraham Lincoln as the ultimate representation of honesty around which to build your company, "Lincoln Financial Services" may sound more professional than "Honest Abe's ATMs." The name should also be unique so that it stands out, is memorable, and your customers can easily find you.

Try to come up with several company names and then spend time researching each. Begin by examining your Secretary of State website to see which names you thought of are available. Pay special attention to any local businesses with similar-sounding names to avoid customer confusion. Next, check if there is a corresponding domain name available. For example, if LincolnFinancial Services.com is available, you are on the right track. Lastly, remember to check all major social media sites to ensure that a suitable username is available.

Once you've selected your name and the theme of your company, you'll need to create your logo. This design is a visual symbol that represents the essence of your brand and should be both professional and unique. Remember, it will be visible on your business cards, website, marketing materials, and email signature, so it's best to design something that will look impressive across all applications. Color is a major consideration when designing a logo. While many financial institutions choose green, as the color of money and prosperity, you may choose to use dark blue, which is viewed as a symbol of trustworthiness and integrity. Ultimately, use your creativity to integrate your name and logo into a professional representation of you and your company.

Taxes

As with any business, a portion of income earned must be set aside to pay taxes. Depending on your state, you are responsible for state and/or federal income tax. States such as Florida and Texas do not have a state income tax where most others do.

Tax preparation differs depending on your business entity. As a new business owner, I recommend hiring a professional to prepare your taxes to ensure that no costly mistakes are made and to remove the time burden from your plate. Time spent acquiring new locations is more valuable than learning how to calculate and file taxes. Fortunately, for ATM businesses, the software provided by your processor keeps track of all income generated by the ATMs that is deposited to your bank account. This simplifies compiling yearly financial data for tax preparation.

One aspect of tax preparation many business owners commonly overlook is the number of deductions available to claim with an ATM business. You may be aware that you can deduct mileage and travel expenses as you drive around for sales meetings or loading your ATMs, but, in reality, a deduction can be claimed for any expenditure designed to generate profit. This includes expenses related to professional services (accounting and legal), repairs and maintenance, marketing, graphic design, office space, health insurance, web hosting, education, and more.

Also, ask your accountant about the depreciation of your ATMs.

Claiming these deductions will increase your profit by reducing your tax burden, so don't be afraid to take a hard look at what you've truly spent on all facets of your business. Chances are, there are many more deductions you can claim than you first realized.

Lastly, if you sell ATMs or parts to locations, investigate whether you need to collect and remit local sales tax.

Remember to consult a tax professional regarding your specific circumstances as the information in this book does not constitute tax advice.

CHAPTER 6

STEP 2 - SETTING UP BANK ACCOUNTS

Whether you choose a sole proprietorship or establish a corporation to run your ATM business, you need to develop a relationship with a local bank and open a bank account. This account is where both the cash used to fill the ATMs (vault cash) and the surcharge income will be deposited and withdrawn. Some business owners choose to open two separate accounts, one for the surcharge income and the other for the vault cash. In either case, attempt to form a strong business relationship with your bank. You will need the bank's cooperation when frequently withdrawing a few thousand dollars in crisp $20 bills in a single transaction.

I emphasize the relationship aspect, because in today's business climate, banks aren't entirely amenable to working with ATM companies. Prior to the 2008 recession, all banks fully supported working with ATM companies. In an effort to minimize the risk of another crash, the government enacted restrictions on banks to rein in their reckless behavior that heavily contribution to wrecking the economy.

Currently, banks take a cautious approach to ATM businesses due to a program called Operation Choke Point, which classified ATM businesses as high risk. This makes it more difficult to find a bank willing to associate with your business. Despite the program ending in late 2017, larger banks such as Chase, Wells Fargo, and Bank of America have steered clear of providing accounts for ATM businesses. To avoid this problem, new ATM businesses should look to smaller local community or international banks to establish accounts. Without endorsing any particular institution, Regions Bank, PNC, and TD Bank are a few banks who have begun working with ATM companies. Fortunately, moving forward, the ATM industry anticipates the lingering impact of Operation Choke Point to wane.

As mentioned above, as a sole proprietor, you can use an established personal account, but if you form an LLC or S corp., it's important to open a business account separate from your personal account.

CHAPTER 7

STEP 3 - ATM PROCESSING AND ATM TRANSACTIONS

In order to begin accepting bank cards and dispensing cash to cardholders at your ATMs, you will need to sign up with an ATM processor. An ATM processor provides the connection between the ATM and the cash withdrawn. While the cardholder is taking out cash while viewing a screen with simple options, copious amounts of information is exchanged behind the scenes.

At a basic level, the ATM communicates with the ATM processor, who then communicates with card networks and banks. The card networks and banks communicate back to the ATM processor, and the processor back to the ATM. The ATM finally dispenses cash and the amount requested plus the surcharge fee is transferred to your bank account from the cardholder's. This entire cycle occurs in a matter of seconds.

Illustrating further, analogous to an Internet Service Provider (ISP), an ATM processor provides the link through which ATM networks are made available to the cardholder. Processors act as a middleman between the ATM and financial institutions. Without an ATM processor, an ATM is rendered purposeless.

Finding a quality ATM processor is integral to the success of your business. In addition to serving as a middleman as described above, ATM processors provide many benefits to ATM businesses to nurture and facilitate their growth. Because a processor is making money on all of your transactions, they are financially incentivized to ensure your success. The more transactions you have processing with their network, the more money they earn. Hence, processors provide all the tools and consultation necessary to help you build your business.

Working with a processor is a partnership in many ways, so it's wise to select a reputable processor that has a history of facilitating growth for both new and mature ATM businesses.

Generally, look for a processor who provides:

- Access to purchase ATMs at wholesale prices
- Real-time reporting through an online portal
- ATM parts and supplies
- Around the clock technical support
- Cash loading solutions

- Wireless units
- Coaching, consulting, and guidance
- Strong back-office support

And as with all services on which you'll be relying to make your business work, look for a processor that is professional, prompt, and communicates well during business hours.

Lastly, you can find an ATM processor using a basic Google search or through a referral. Notwithstanding, the best way is to venture to an area with a few independent ATMs, locate the sticker on the bottom half of the ATM, and make note of the processing company.

The Flow of an ATM Transaction

In the previous section, we learned the mechanics of an ATM transaction from the vantage point of the ATM processor. However, for more clarity, it's important to understand the flow of a transaction from an ATM owner's business perspective.

Step 1: You provide the ATM and cash in the ATM for customers to withdraw.

Step 2: Connect the ATM to the processing network.

Step 3: A cardholder inserts his/her card and requests cash from the ATM.

Step 4: The ATM communicates the request for cash to the ATM processor.

Step 5: The ATM processor determines if the funds are available from the customer's bank and gets approval to proceed with the transaction.

Step 6: The ATM dispenses the cash and a paper or electronic receipt.

Step 7: Finally, the amount of cash withdrawn and surcharge fee are transferred from the customer's bank account to your bank account. Funds will appear the following business day.

How to make Money: Surcharge and Interchange

There are two primary income streams an ATM owner collects as revenue in the ATM business. The surcharge fee and interchange.

The surcharge the fee is paid by the cardholder in order to withdraw cash. This is the primary method of earning revenue. The cardholder inserts his/her card and accepts the surcharge fee to withdraw cash from his/her account. On the low end, surcharge fees are $2 to $3 per transaction, and on the high end, $10 or even 10%. This number is influenced by the type of location and strength of demand for cash.

Interchange is a small fee earned by ATM processors on each transaction at the machine. Processors receive this fee for all the transaction types including, but not limited to, withdrawals, balance checks, or denials. Because ATM processors conveniently act as middlemen to countless financial institutions, banks are happy to pay this fee, which ranges from, $.01 to $.40 per transaction.

The amount of the interchange varies with each transaction depending on a variety of factors including, but not limited to, the merchant industry, the type of card (debit or credit), transaction size, and geographic location.

Initially, the ATM processor is entitled to keep most, if not all, of the interchange to cover expensive network fees and costs. However, once your business reaches a significant amount of total monthly transactions – around 10,000 – a processor will begin sharing a portion of the interchange with you.

CHAPTER 8

STEP 4 - ATM LOCATIONS AND ROUTE BUILDING

Finding ATM Locations

The main question to address when starting an ATM business is: where are you going to place your ATMs? Similar to real estate, the quality of locations is the key to earning income from ATMs. The two most important factors in scouting ATM locations are a strong demand for cash and high foot traffic. Both factors increase the likelihood of producing a high volume of transactions and high revenues.

ATMs continue to thrive in locations such as: any place that does not accept cards, 24-hour establishments, hotels, condos, gas stations, convenience stores, liquor stores, laundromats, high tourist areas, restaurants, bars, arcades, tow yards, large salons, tattoo parlors, night clubs, gentlemen's clubs, marijuana dispensaries, parking garages, and more.

First and foremost, a business owner must adopt the mindset that an ATM placement is an investment. Therefore, the primary aim is to find places where the profit will exceed the investment costs in a reasonable amount of time. For example, let's say your initial investment into a machine and vault cash is $4,000. You agree with the owner to charge $3 for a transaction of which you keep $2.50 and pay the owner $.50. After three months, your ATM is averaging 50 transactions per month, earning you an average of $125 in profit per month ($2.50 * 50). Dividing your initial investment of $4,000 by $125, you discover it will take 32 months to recoup your costs. Now, if you divide $125 by $4,000, the result is 0.03125, which if you convert to a percentage, equals 3.125%. 3.125% represents the percentage profit per month on your initial investment of $4,000. From a yearly perspective, you are earning 37.5%. If you think this sounds too good to be true, you are mistaken, as this is an example of a low performing location.

Alternatively, if your ATM is in an extremely high traffic and cash demand area, your initial investment increases to $5,500 because you utilize $3,000 to fill the machine. The ATM averages 300 transactions in a month and, at $2.50, you'll earn $750 in profit that month. Here, your investment is recouped in just over seven months. What's more, you are now earning 13.6% per month on your investment. That's 163% annually!

It's important to remember that revenue isn't the same thing as profit. Profit is revenue minus expenses. Your expenses will include the cost of the ATM, cash used to fill it, commission paid to the location, and potentially a wireless box.

*At the end of this chapter, we provide you with a chart that helps break down common location types providing the pros and cons of each.

Qualities of Strong ATM Locations

When considering what types of locations are best suited for an ATM, there are certain qualities that you should seek. A strong location, where a steady stream of transactions occurs daily, is vital to maximizing profit for your ATM business.

The first and most important quality of a strong ATM location is profit potential. High foot traffic, demand for cash (cash only), open 24/7, and alcohol consumption are classic indicators of locations with high profit potential. Locations where locals and tourists flock to, including downtowns, shopping, and restaurant districts, are ideal. These areas are hotspots for plenty of hotels, nightclubs, and bars where people traditionally need and spend cash.

Further, markets, convenience stores, and gas stations are also traditionally high profit locations, producing a steady flow of predictable transactions.

The second quality for a strong ATM location is ease of ATM management. Is there quick and easy access to the ATM? Ideally, for loading and maintenance purposes, the location is in a safe neighborhood that is easy to access, convenient for parking, and open long hours (ideally 24/7). Another consideration is the method the location chooses to receive its commission payments. No commission locations and direct deposit locations are the easiest to manage, followed by locations asking for quarterly or monthly payments by check.

The final important quality to consider is long-term stability. Your goal is to have your ATM thrive in a given location in perpetuity. You don't want to find yourself in a situation where a location is in jeopardy mere months after acquiring it. Reasons a location might be in jeopardy shortly after acquiring it include a change of ownership (turnover), a short or weak agreement, and, most notably, abundant competition due to the location being highly desirable.

Here are some tips for maintaining stability. The first way to mitigate the risk of losing a location is to create a long, mutually beneficial agreement containing an exclusivity clause and assignment/buyout clause. Logically, it's important to sign longer-term agreements, typically three or more years with an auto-renewal clause. Next, an exclusivity clause will prevent the competition from trying to undercut your prices while simultaneously holding the owner accountable to follow through with the terms of the agreement. The exclusivity clause ensures a competing ATM cannot be installed on the premises without breaching your agreement. After all, an owner does not want potentially to entangle himself in a costly and time-consuming legal predicament.

Next, for protection against high turnover businesses or if the owner sells the business to a third-party, an assignment/buyout clause dictates that if the ATM agreement is not assumed by the purchasing business, the current owner must pay you damages in the form of a lump sum buyout. Turnover is the term used when a business is sold, surrendered due to debt, or in any way changes ownership or management. In general, nightclubs have the highest turnover rate due to the high cost of operation and unpredictable customer base. In our experience with various nightclubs, our ATMs have lasted anywhere from six months to five years. By contrast, apartment buildings have a very low turnover rate. They are infrequently bought or sold, management typically remains consistent, and the barrier to entry is high, preventing competitors from bombarding the management with proposals.

Working with a reliable and trustworthy owner is also paramount for stability. Be on the lookout for red flags. One sign of an unreliable owner is difficulty with communication. If you're unable to reach the owner reliably over phone or email, you may find yourself in a position where you weren't alerted promptly to a down machine. Further, you want to avoid owners who are constantly on the prowl for a better deal and who wouldn't hesitate to attempt to cancel or renegotiate the agreement.

You want to create strong relationships with owners by building rapport as it's the best tool to ensure long-term prosperity at a location. Expertly managing the ATM, paying commissions timely, and being prompt in keeping your machine online and filled is vital. Also, being friendly and communicative with the staff and management builds trust, loyalty, and goodwill, such that the owner will think twice about switching to a new service provider once the agreement expires. Deep trust and goodwill may even lead to referral opportunities, where you become the ATM provider for the owners' friends and business acquaintances.

The following are the most common types of ATM locations and evaluations of the qualities to consider. Your local area may have a wider variety of potential locations than found on this list that are suitable for ATMs, but this list is a smart place to begin your search.

	Type of Location	Profit Potential	Ease of Management	Stability
1	Nightclub	Strong	Low	Low
2	Bar	Maybe	High	Yes
3	Restaurant	Maybe	High	Maybe
4	Parking garage	Strong	High	Yes
5	Salon	Maybe	High	Yes
6	Grocery market	Strong	High	Yes
7	Arcade	Strong	High	Yes
8	Apartment building	Strong	High	Yes
9	Hotel	Strong	High	Yes
10	Hostel	Strong	High	Yes
11	Marijuana dispensary	Strong	High	Maybe
12	Mall	Strong	High	Maybe
13	Car wash	Maybe	High	Yes
14	Gas station	Strong	High	Low
15	Convenience/Liquor store	Strong	High	Yes
16	Tow yard	Strong	High	Yes
17	Events/Mobile ATM	Strong	Low	Yes

18	Currency exchange	Maybe	High	Yes
19	Strip club/ Gentlemen's club	Strong	Low	Low
20	Laundromat	Strong	High	Yes

Building a Safe and Manageable Route

Because you will be filling your ATMs with your cash, at least early on, it's best practice to create a safe and easy-to-manage loading route. Typically, most ATM owners aim to load each ATM once a week, loading all ATMs within one or two days. To complete loading efficiently consider the following strategies:

1. **Attempt to minimize the distance between locations, since driving from location to location encompasses the majority of your total loading time.** You'll want them to be as close in proximity as possible. If they are spread out throughout the region, plan on spending more time on the road and on gas, and less time acquiring new locations.

2. **Target locations with easy parking and quick access to the ATM.** Parking close is essential for not wasting time and for safety. You will be carrying several thousand dollars in cash for loading, so it's best to be expedient.

3. **Talk to your location owner about the best way to access the ATM for loading and maintenance.** Maybe entering through a side employee entrance will grant quicker access to the machine versus entering through the front door. The idea is to enter and exit as swiftly as possible.

4. **Lastly, keep in mind locations' hours.** If a location is open around the clock seven days a week like a hotel or condo, you have wide flexibility for your loading schedule. On the other hand, a nightclub with limited hours and open only three nights a week presents scheduling and access challenges.

CHAPTER 9

STEP 5 - SALES, DEALS, AND AGREEMENTS

Basics: How to Find and Sign Deals with New Locations

There are many strategies and techniques to employ for attempting to secure new locations, some basic and some advanced. Best practice is to utilize as many as necessary in harmony to maximize success.

The process of sales and signing new locations requires a major shift in your mindset. To succeed in this business, you must constantly be thinking about selling to and acquiring locations. Throughout your normal daily routines, shopping for groceries, dining out with the family, stopping for gas, or meeting a friend at a bar, your mind must always be considering would an ATM succeed in this business? If yes, does the location currently have an ATM? If so, what type of machine? Is it new or old; is it compliant? Is the ATM out of cash? Maybe the location isn't being paid on time or enough? How can I gain access to a decision-maker? This general thought process allows you to visualize opportunities and develop strategies to win business. Importantly, do not disregard or disqualify a location because it already houses an ATM. It's possible that commission payments are consistently late, or the ATM is left without money for long stretches; this information gives you leverage to earn the account. Ultimately, you are going to sell them on providing a more well-rounded and profitable solution than their current situation.

I presume that in the course of reading this book, or even prior, your mind has been generating ideas for locations to pursue. Everyone encounters locations in their daily lives that are ideal candidates for an ATM placement. The first step is to approach these locations and inquire about their ATM situation with a decision-maker. Think about what locations you routinely visit? A local gas station or bar perhaps? These are ideal scenarios to begin with due to your familiarity with the location.

In addition to beginning with familiar local locations, start by taking advantage of your inner circle. Do you know anyone who works or manages a bar, hotel, or supermarket? Inquiring with people who already know and trust you is an easier path with fewer obstacles to launching your business. Reach out to these connections and let them know how you can help their businesses with your ATM service.

Once you've investigated and pursued familiar locations in your daily life and maximized your personal connections, the next step is to decide what type of establishments and geographic area to target. If you decide targeting hotels will be most fruitful for you, find as many hotels within a desired radius and map them out by neighborhood. Canvas the neighborhoods by walking or driving through to scout for potential sites. Make sure to note any potential locations and obtain their contact information (found on signs or website) to get in touch. If practicable, enter the locations and speak with the decision-maker about their particular ATM situation. If a decision-maker is unavailable, leave a business card and a flyer explaining who you are and what services you offer. Don't forget to follow up after a few days to ascertain their interest.

In unison with physical canvasing, begin reaching out to potential locations in the area by cold calling. Gather your list of hotels or restaurants and find the contact numbers for each. You simply call or email the business and ask to speak to a decision-maker. Discuss their interest in having an ATM to provide access to cash for their customers. Be sure you focus on all the ways the business will benefit from your ATM. Cold calling is an accelerated form of canvassing. However, face-to-face interaction is usually more effective than phone communication. The best practice with cold calling is to schedule an in-person meeting with a decision-maker.

These are the basic strategies to employ when beginning with zero locations. Toward the end of this book, we will discuss more advanced strategies for scaling up once you have established clients and a reputable company.

Advantages of Housing an ATM for a Business

There are three primary reasons why a location owner will benefit from making cash available to its customers with an ATM. Be sure to make these points known to hesitant or skeptical owners during your sales pitch.

1. **Increased traffic and in-store spending (gas stations, markets, convenience stores, bars, nightclubs, restaurants).**

   On average, 40% of regular ATM users will use an ATM 8-10 times per month. Of those transactions, at least 25% of the cash withdrawn is generally spent on the premises. For bars, clubs, and restaurants, it can be as high as 75% of the cash withdrawn spent at the location. Further, customers who use ATMs tend to spend 20% to 25% more than non-ATM users. Lastly, stores with ATMs have historically seen an increase in sales and in-store spending by at least 8% due to increased traffic.

Use these statistics to demonstrate that the value of an ATM goes beyond merely earning a residual income stream and convenience for customers. Conclusively, the presence of an ATM leads to higher foot traffic and in-store spending.

2. Lower credit card fees and reduced chargebacks.

In exchange for the ability to accept credit cards for payments, businesses must pay a fee to the credit card processor. The typical fees range from 2%-3% of the total transaction. For example, American Express charges close to 3% to accept its cards. On a $100 transaction, $3 is deducted and paid to American Express leaving the business owner with $97.

Now let's say the business has an ATM and earns $1 per transaction. Instead of charging the American Express card, the business suggests the customer withdraw cash from the ATM. The business profits $1 on the ATM transaction and simultaneously saves $3 on the credit card fees. Here, a $100 purchase nets the business $101 instead of $97. After 100 transactions, this $4 results in $400 more cash for the business.

3. Earn residual income.

As explained throughout this book, whether through a free placement or purchasing an ATM, a business will earn profit every time a customer withdraws cash. Ultimately, additional passive income is the primary draw for a business.

Placement and Processing Deals

There are two distinct methods of earning money in the ATM business; placement deals and processing. Thus far, in all of our examples, we've learned the ins and outs Placement deals as they are employed most frequently. To reiterate, a Placement is an arrangement where the ATM owner leases a space in a commercial location to install and operate an ATM. You compensate the location owner for the use of their space via a portion of the surcharge income generated at the machine. A common portrayal of a Placement Deal structure is charging $3 to withdraw cash and compensating the owner $1.

With Placements, you own the ATM and are responsible for loading your cash. Likewise, you are solely responsible for maintaining and operating the machine. The business owner bears no responsibility as they don't own the ATM. You'll visit the machine each time it needs to be filled with cash or serviced and pay the location owner monthly or quarterly.

The second method of earning money from ATMs is through Processing. Processing is where you earn money by processing transactions rather than from the surcharge fee. Under this arrangement, the location owns the ATM and uses its own cash for cardholders to withdraw. The location either purchased an ATM in the past or purchases one from you. For example, a grocery store opts to purchase an ATM from you and manage it themselves with their own cash while you provide the connection for processing enabling the ATM to function.

With both Placements and Processing arrangements at your disposal, you have a complete arsenal of tools to adapt to the needs of any location. Processing works well to supplement existing Placement ATMs to increase your profitability. Since you are already directly connected to a processor, simply charge business owners a small processing fee to connect to your network. This saves the owner the trouble and expense of setting up its own network account and gives you a completely task-free income. Best of all, you only have to visit these ATMs if the machine needs service.

Understanding these two business models and how they overlap is vital to your success. The following section will delve deeper into the mechanics of how to use these arrangements creatively to tackle any ATM location.

The Four Models of ATM Deals

Now that you have a firm understanding of Placement and Processing business models, here are four ways to structure deals when approaching a business. This section breaks down Placement and Processing to fit the needs of any location.

1. **The first is Full Placement.** As described in previous chapters, you own and operate an ATM in a third-party location. A business benefits from this arrangement by earning a percentage of the income earned at the ATM, without any direct involvement.

   Initially, this model is the most expensive launch because it requires, on average, $4,000 to $6,000 in startup capital for a new ATM, installation costs, and ongoing cash to load. Notwithstanding, purchasing a used machine is an option for lower volume locations to minimize startup costs, but keep in mind that locations may prefer a new machine due to the aesthetics of the location.

2. **The second structure is Partial Placement.** Partial Placements are a derivative of Full Placements with one tweak. Under this arrangement, you own the ATM while the location, not you, is responsible for loading the cash. This method is beneficial for the ATM owner because it saves loading costs and puts the management on autopilot. The location benefits by receiving a higher commission for keeping the ATM filled with cash. The most common commission split for a Partial Placement is 50/50. If the surcharge fee is $3, you earn $1.50, and the location earns $1.50.

3. **The third deal structure is Processing.** As discussed previously, the location owns and loads their own ATM, and you provide the processing network, monitoring software, and maintenance. You earn money by selling a machine to the location at a markup price for a profit and from processing fees. Benefits for you include zero upfront capital is required, and the ATM operation is completely hands off. The downside is that processing income alone is minimal compared income earned from a Placement. A location benefits by earning the entire surcharge fee minus the processing fee, but also bears the total responsibility of loading.

4. **A common variation to basic Processing is where the location owns the ATM but hires**

you to load and maintain it. In this situation, again, you sell the location an ATM, and you are responsible for loading the cash. You earn a loading fee in addition to earning processing fees. For example, in exchange for keeping the ATM filled with cash, you earn a $1 per transaction loading fee. If the location does 200 transactions in a month, you'd earn $200. If you allocate $4,000 to the ATM, that $200 is a 5% profit on your total loading costs each month ($200 profit / $4,000 principle = 5%). Earning 5% each month for 12 months results in 60% profit in a year.

Persuading Businesses to Switch to Your Company

If a business already has an ATM, why should they switch to YOUR ATM company? After all, any worthwhile location has likely been approached by other ATM companies in the past. This is where you'll need to emphasize the benefits of working with you, including your impeccable service track record, on time payments, and overall dependability. Anyone can entice an owner by dangling a brand-new ATM. However, you can separate yourself from the pack with a story of how well your customers are accommodated. Owners want to feel that you're attending to their every need. One underutilized technique is to collect testimonials from your current customers that you can share with potential new clients. Testimonials represent social proof attesting to your company's capabilities that will propel you over the competition in the eyes of owners.

Signing a new client to your processing services may be slightly more challenging. If you're approaching a location that currently has an ATM machine, how do you persuade the owner to switch to your processing network? The following are the important points with which to focus your pitch to a prospective processing client:

First, offer to meet or beat the business' current income by offering a lower processing fee. If the surcharge is $3 and the processor is keeping $.25, offer another $.15 profit by keeping only $.10. It's important to remember as a processor, if you have enough transactions, you will earn a share of the interchange fee. Thus, if the location is charging $3, you can offer for them to keep the entire $3 while still earning the interchange fee.

The next focus should be on your dependability. Stress your outstanding service, customer support, response time, and availability. Explain that you and your team are available not only during business hours but also after hours in case of an emergency. Convince the owner that as his/her ATM service provider, you will provide the utmost care and attention to detail.

Lastly, it's quite common for a location that owns their own ATM to not have upgraded the machine in a number of years. As the years pass, old machines become more unreliable and malfunction more frequently. Further, as the legal and banking industries evolve change, ATM compliance with those evolutions becomes a factor. Within the past decade, ADA (Americans with Disabilities Act) and EMV (Europay, MasterCard, and Visa) compliance have forced ATM manufacturers to make necessary changes to their ATMs to comply.

ADA compliance is a federal law ensuring people with disabilities are equally able to withdraw cash from ATMs. Changes to ATMs include adding Braille instructions and voice guidance for the visually impaired and adjusting the height of the ATM and screen for those in wheelchairs.

EMV compliance is related to the banking industry shifting to a more secure form of card data storage. All new bank and credit cards contain a chip embedded in the plastic to store your data rather than using the magnetic stripe. New ATMs are equipped with redesigned card readers to read data from the chips.

ADA and EMV compliance will be discussed in deeper depth later in this book.

Consequently, older outdated ATMs require patchwork and costly additional parts and labor to reach new compliance standards. Hence, in these situations, the selling point is that new machines are dependable and fully compliant out of the box. And as the incentive to purchase from you, offer to purchase their old ATM at market value and credit the purchase price toward the purchase of a new ATM. For example, if a new ATM costs $2,500, and you purchase the old machine for $1,000, the location will only need to spend $1,500 on a new ATM. This way, the customer receives a heavily discounted new compliant ATM while giving you an extra used ATM for a new location.

Setting Yourself Up for Maximum Profit

Obviously, it's in your best interest to ensure you are maximizing profit potential with each ATM you place in the field. There are two factors to maximize your profit; first, setting the right surcharge fee, and second, negotiating the best commission split. The surcharge-to-commission ratio is your direct line to profit, so it's imperative to optimize both numbers.

Typically, out-of-network banks charge $3 to withdraw cash, so $3 is used as a rule of thumb as an amount to charge at your independent ATMs. Raise or lower your surcharge in direct proportion to demand for cash and volume.

With a $3 surcharge, aim for a 75/25 split with the location. Here you profit $2.25 on each transaction while the location receives $0.75. Initially, from a negotiating standpoint, offer as close to a $3/$0 split as possible. Every location should be evaluated independently based on the unique circumstances, but generally agreeing to a lower than 50/50 split won't be profitable for you. If at 50/50, propose raising the surcharge to $3.25 or $3.50 to maximize profit.

Some ATM owners find they can squeeze out more profit if they use a performance-based tiered structure for their commission split. Here's an example of how that would work, still using $3 as the assumed surcharge rate:

- For the first 99 transactions, the ATM owner would get $2.50, while the location owner would get $0.50.
- For transactions 100 to 199, the split would be $2.00 and $1.00.
- For transactions 200+, the split would be $1.50 and $1.50.

The reason this model is successful is that location owners often overestimate anticipated transaction volume. Once they realize their ATM transaction volume is falling short of expectations, they'll become incentivized to start driving traffic to the ATM. With more traffic coming in, you might be paying a slightly higher commission, but you'll reap the rewards of more traffic.

Another variety of commission split to consider is to pay the location owner 0% for the first 50 transactions, and 50% on any transactions after 50. This is a savvy way to ensure profit from an ATM in a lower traffic area where 50 or 100 transactions per month is difficult to reach.

Finally, consider entering into flat-fee agreements with locations. For example, lease your ATM to the location owner for a flat $300 per month while the location owner keeps all the profit generated from the surcharge. Here, you can count on receiving that $300 every month regardless of the transaction volume. When attempting to negotiate this arrangement, emphasize that potential earnings after $300 is unlimited. This structure also motivates owners to drive traffic to the ATM.

The chart below shows some common commission splits and how much your company will profit per month for 50, 100, 150, and 200 transactions (still assuming a $3 surcharge):

# Transactions	50	100	150	200
50/50 after 50	$150	$225	$300	$375
$2.50 / $0.50	$125	$250	$375	$500
$2.25 / $0.75	$112.50	$225	$337.50	$450
$2 / $1	$100	$200	$300	$400

Return on Investment

To get the best return on your investment, striking the right balance between profit margin and volume is paramount. Profit margin is the amount earned after paying commission to the location owner. The higher your margin, the fewer transactions you need to make your return on investment. For example, in a given month, if you have 50 transactions at a $2 margin, you make the same amount of income as with 100 transactions at a $1 margin. Given that the ATM has a higher probability of doing 50 transactions in a month than 100, locking in a $2 margin is vital. Also, a smaller number of transactions is easier to manage because you won't have to load as often and fill it with as much cash.

This is one area where purchasing a used machine is advantageous. Used machines cost significantly less than the price of a new machine. Utilizing a used ATM allows you to recoup your initial investment faster and start earning pure profit sooner.

Importance of a Signed Agreement

A common question posed by new ATM business owners is whether it's necessary to obtain a signed agreement for each location. The short and wise answer is yes because agreements outline rights and protections for both parties in the event a complication arises. Without an agreement, there is no documentation to help settle disputes. Initiating legal recourse is viewed as an option of last resort as it's confrontational and expensive for both parties. Ergo, having a document to refer to helps prevent this.

Further, having a clear, fair, and thorough agreement in writing helps create an initial standard of trust between the parties, and it serves as a foundation for a strong business relationship.

Additionally, agreements fortify business certainty. If your agreement permits you to operate your ATM in a location for five years, you safely can forecast five years of profit for that location. Ultimately, agreements ensure both parties are protected, and they fortify the business relationship.

Having said that, there are rare instances where owners prefer not to sign an agreement at all. However, don't perceive this is a deal-breaker. If you build rapport with the owner and management, manage the machine professionally, and pay commissions on time, ownership will not look to replace you.

What to Include in ATM Agreements

There are several important provisions to include in your ATM agreements. At a minimum, agreements should include:

- **A definition of the landlord-tenant relationship.** With an ATM placement, you are leasing a space from the landlord/owner to place and operate an ATM. A lease arrangement offers you additional rights, which vary from state to state.
- **The legal names of both parties** to ensure that the agreement is valid and enforceable.
- **The duration of the agreement.** Most ATM agreements are set for three to five years and have an auto-renew period of the same length. The goal is to recoup the initial investment cost in the shortest time possible. Having a multi-year agreement allows you to maximize the profitability from a location once the initial investment is recouped.
- **A clearly defined commission split.** Each party should know how much of the surcharge they will earn and the frequency of payment.
- **A statement of ownership of the ATM.** Clearly state which party holds the ownership rights to the ATM.
- **A statement of exclusivity.** If the location allows a competitor to place an ATM on the premises or removes yours, the agreement is violated. Under the agreement, you will have legal recourse.

- **A buyout option.** In most cases, the location owner will have a period of 36 months to void the agreement for any reason, cancel the service, and have the ATM removed. If the owner elects to cancel, you are entitled to the buyout fee described in the agreement. This clause protects you from unpredictable ownership, allowing you to recoup your investment costs while also giving the owner an appearance of freedom from being trapped into an agreement.

At Acme, we provide custom agreements to all our clients for free. We also sell custom agreements to non-clients on our website. If you need a ready-made agreement that covers all the bases written by professionals with plenty of experience, please visit ATMResidualIncome.com.

CHAPTER 10

STEP 6 - ATM PURCHASING DECISIONS

Purchasing ATMs

Once you've secured a location to place an ATM, the next step is to decide what kind of ATM to purchase. There are a few considerations before purchasing a machine:

Decision #1: New Machine vs. Used Machine

On average, a brand-new ATM will cost $2,500, including taxes and freight shipping. Fortunately, ATM prices have dropped significantly over the years. Just 10 years ago, ATMs were $1,000-$2000 costlier than they are today. Price notwithstanding, there are many reasons why it's practical to purchase new.

- **Longevity:** A new machine will last 7 to 10 years with heavy use. Over that time span, your $2,500 goes a long way.

- **Reliability:** A new machine is far less prone to breaking down or malfunctioning. This minimizes the amount of time and cost related to maintenance, thereby, maximizing potential profit.

- **Compliance:** New ATMs are ADA and EMV chip compliant from the manufacturer. A used ATM will likely require an EMV upgrade kit to replace the old card reader. These kits are costly and negate the purpose of spending less on a used ATM.

- **Aesthetics:** New ATMs are clean and modern, enabling them to stand out aesthetically in any location. Studies show new machines attract more customers, even in locations where a used ATM would be suitable.

- **Ease of Use/Speed of Transaction:** Newer large bright touchscreens and faster internal processors make transactions easier and quicker for the customer. Clunky software and hardware on used machines can hinder transactions.

- **Warranty:** New ATMs come with a factory warranty on parts. If a part breaks within the warranty period, the manufacturer will replace the part for free. On the other hand, if a part breaks on an old machine, the cost of a replacement part will be your responsibility.

- **Newest Tech (NFC and Remote Monitoring):** Some new ATMs come with tech such as NFC (near field communication) and remote monitoring. NFC allows customers to withdraw cash using their smartphones. Remote monitoring allows ATM errors, such as bill jams, to be fixed remotely without visiting the machine.

On the other hand, a used ATM will cost anywhere from $500-$1500 depending on its age, condition, and compliance. The primary advantage of purchasing used ATMs is reduced initial cost of investment, thus, placing used ATMs in slower locations is smart. Buying a used machine is similar to buying a used car in that you must do your due diligence. A seller may clean the outside of the ATM, but internally, parts may be rusty or in poor shape. And with parts not covered by a factory warranty, servicing used machines can get expensive quickly, negating the initial cost savings. Lastly, used ATMs are unlikely to be EMV compliant.

Decision #2: Where to Buy Your ATM

The two primary ways to purchase a new ATM are through your processor or from an online store. Your processor will offer a discount compared to online stores because it commits to buying many ATMs per month. Additionally, a processor, such as Acme ATM, will offer discounts to current and new processing clients. Regardless of where you shop, it's wise to order ATMs from the same manufacturer to simplify service and maintenance. For example, buying all Hyosung Halo 2s or all Genmega 2500s.

Decision #3: What Features and Specs to Choose

Most ATMs are built to last 7-10 years, so it's important to future-proof when ordering. For example, buying ATMs in 2015 without EMV card readers to save money was a mistake as it's now industry standard and mandatory. Here are the basic features your ATMs should have:

- **ADA compliance:** Fortunately, all new ATMs are ADA compliant.
- **EMV card reader:** Recently all manufacturers began including EMV card readers on all machines. Older ATMs must be upgraded to EMV by swapping out the magnetic strip reader for a dip style.
- **1000 note removable cassette:** A 1000 note removable cassette comfortably holds $18,000 in $20 bills. The ability to remove the cassette from the ATM allows you to fill the cassette with cash in a private area rather than at the machine in public.

- **Electronic lock:** Opt for an electronic lock with a 6-digit password rather than a standard dial lock. E-locks are far simpler to set up and use than a dial lock. A dial lock offers no safety advantage over electronic. Lastly, an e-lock streamlines your cash loading because they are quicker to open.

- **Screen display:** While it's tempting to upgrade to a larger screen size, the smaller standard sized screen is more than adequate. All new ATMs are equipped with at least 10.1" color LCD screens, which is larger than they were 5-10 years ago.

- **Topper:** A topper is a marketing sign that reads "ATM" at the top of the machine. The purpose is for potential customers to locate the ATM from a distance. There is no concrete data suggesting a correlation between a topper and increased monthly transactions, but it can't hurt. Unless a location demands it, opt not to purchase a topper. However, a nightlife setting is one where a topper may be helpful.

- **Security camera:** In most cases, it's unnecessary to purchase a built-in security camera because your ATM will be under your location's camera supervision. The ATM will also be bolted to the floor, and any attempt to break into or steal a bolted machine will certainly draw the attention of location attendants and customers.

The final consideration is shipping. Once you've selected your ATM and features, freight shipping from the factory takes 5-10 business days and is usually included in the price of the ATM.

EMV

In the previous chapter, we mentioned that all new ATM machines have been updated with EMV card readers – but what exactly is EMV, and how does it affect ATM businesses?

Traditionally, credit and debit cards were implanted with a magnetic stripe on the back to store card holders' account information. Card readers were only capable of extracting the data from the stripe to conduct transactions. However, due to a growing concern surrounding identity theft and fraud, card companies developed more secure microchips to store the data rather than on magnetic stripes.

Developed and named after a coalition of Europay, MasterCard, and Visa, EMV is simply a tiny chip embedded in payment cards. EMV chips have dynamic encryption capabilities making them virtually impossible to counterfeit and steal information from. Magnetic stripes on the other hand, store static data that is far easier to steal.

Countries in Europe and Asia began migrating to EMV almost a decade before the United States. According to The Federal Reserve, since the beginning of adoption of EMV in participating countries, the United States is the only country where card fraud continues to grow. In 2012, Alaric found that even though the United States represents 23.5% of total card volume worldwide, it accounted for 47.3% of total fraud losses.[1]

Due to EMV dramatically reducing card fraud in participating countries, the United States began formally adopting the standard in 2015. Complete migration is taking years to complete because of the high costs and the many parties involved. Banks must upgrade all debit and credit cards to more expensive chip cards, while merchants and ATM operators must upgrade their card readers to EMV compliant models.

Notwithstanding, migration in the United States is happening in an ongoing manner. To accelerate EMV adoption, Visa and MasterCard both enacted card fraud liability shift deadlines, October 2016 and October 2017 respectively. Subsequent to these deadlines, any party operating an ATM without an EMV compliant card reader and software is liable for any fraud occurring at their noncompliant terminal.

According to EMVCo, the main organization facilitating EMV migration worldwide, implementing liability shift deadlines somewhat succeeded, as EMV adoption in the United States reached nearly 60% by

---

[1] https://www.paymentscardsandmobile.com/wp-content/uploads/2015/03/PCM_Alaric_Fraud-Report_2015.pdf

the end of 2017, with 785 million EMV cards in circulation.[2] A study by Visa published in May 2019 asserts that in March 2019, 99% of card-present Visa transactions were with EMV cards.[3]

Demonstrating the efficacy of EMV, the same Visa study maintains that card-present fraud decreased by 76% for fully EMV compliant merchants from September 2015 to December 2018.

For ATM owners to migrate to EMV, they must upgrade from magnetic card readers to EMV card readers if the ATM is upgradable. If the ATM is not upgradable, the ATM needs to be replaced. The ATM owner must also install the latest software allowing the ATM to conduct EMV transactions.

Similar to the ADA requirements, ATM owners must balance the costs of upgrading or replacing ATMs against the potential losses from fraud liability. The cost of an EMV upgrade kit ranges from $300-$750, depending on the make, model, and year the ATM was manufactured. The software is easily downloadable from websites of ATM processors, manufacturers, and resellers. As discussed previously, any newly purchased ATM is fully upgraded – hardware and software.

---

[2] https://www.creditcardinsider.com/learn/chip-and-signature-chip-and-pin-emv-cards/
[3] https://usa.visa.com/visa-everywhere/blog/bdp/2019/05/28/chip-technology-helps-1559068467332.html

CHAPTER 11

STEP 7 - PROGRAM AND INSTALL AN ATM

Programming an ATM

Programming an ATM is the process of connecting the machine to the processing network and banks to conduct transactions. Both new and used ATMs require programming, or reprogramming, to connect the ATM to a processor assigned terminal ID. A terminal ID is a unique identifying ID assigned by a processor to the type of ATM, specific location, and bank accounts used for surcharge collection and vault replenishment.

To connect an ATM to terminal ID, one must bind keys into the ATM, which means entering serial numbers from secure tamper-evident mailer-like documents called comvelopes. This allows the ATM to communicate with the customer's bank to withdraw cash and deposit the corresponding amount into the ATM owner's account.

Programming can take place before installing the ATM at the location or once installed, it's a matter of preference.

Where to Install an ATM Onsite

The best spot in the location to install your ATM is one that's highly visible, easily accessible by customers, heavily trafficked, and close to a free electrical outlet. For optimal usage, consider installing by the restrooms, near the entrance, in the lobby, by the mailboxes, near the bar, by the concessions, and near the payment point. After selecting a spot, determine if there is enough space around the ATM for the vault door to swing open wide enough so it can easily be loaded and managed.

If confronted with the option or opportunity to place an ATM inside or outside, inside is nearly always the preferred choice. Not only is the machine safer, it also prevents wear and tear or damage from wind, rain, or snow.

If the location calls for an outdoor machine, you can purchase an enclosure to keep your machine safe. However, outdoor enclosures are expensive costing around $2,000.

Preparing for Installation and Bolting ATM to the Floor or Wall

In virtually every situation, you will secure the ATM by bolting it into the floor or wall (for wall-mounted machines). This ensures the machine is safe from theft, making it almost impossible to steal.

Before bolting, it's important to clear the install area of all debris. Next, make sure that ADA requirements are met by allowing enough space for customers with wheelchairs or other mobility aids to have access to the ATM. Move the ATM to the installation spot, open the cabinet vault door to find the four pre-drilled holes in the corners. Using a pencil or Sharpie, mark the holes for drilling onto the floor. Once measured and aligned, move the ATM off the spot and begin drilling into the floor. After drilling, clear the area of all debris with a broom or vacuum. Next, move the ATM back into position by aligning the traced holes with drilled holes and insert, hammer, and fasten the anchor bolts to secure the ATM to the spot.

For most locations, this task will require a concrete drill bit and concrete anchor bolts. If you're unable to anchor a machine into concrete or tile yourself, consider hiring a professional service that has all the tools and experience necessary for a successful installation.

Connection Types

Once the ATM is physically installed, the next phase is to connect the ATM to the network. For an ATM to connect to the processing network, there must be one of three connections available. These are the methods used to connect an ATM to the processor:

1. **Phone line:** Similar to the ancient dial-up internet service, an ATM machine can be connected to the processor via phone line. This is the least preferred method of connection because it's slow, costly, and will not work if the line is occupied by a call. Don't be surprised to see overall transaction volume hampered by a phone line connection. Ultimately, dedicated phone lines are a lose/lose scenario for the both the ATM owner and location.

2. **Internet:** If the ATM location has broadband internet access, connect the ATM to its network through ethernet cable. This is the preferred connection method because transactions are fast, secure, and reliable. Also, there is no cost to the ATM owner.

3. **Wireless box:** Wireless boxes are small, easy-to-install boxes that carry an AT&T or Verizon cellular signal to the ATM. After local internet, this is the next preferred type of

connection because transactions are extremely fast, secure, and reliable. If a box malfunctions for any reason, the processor can reset the box remotely. If a box becomes inoperable, because the boxes are under warranty, simply mail it to the processor in exchange for a new one for free. The only downside of using wireless boxes is the cost, which is around $20 per month.

CHAPTER 12

STEP 8 - FILL THE ATM WITH CASH

Who Loads Cash into the ATM

There are three different arrangements an ATM owner can utilize to have an ATM filled with cash. In most cases, the ATM owner uses their own cash and fills the ATM as needed. However, you may choose to organize your business in a different way.

The second option is to hire a third-party to load the machine in your place. Professional loading services provide the cash investment and fill your machines as needed, saving you startup costs and time. This service typically costs anywhere from $.75 to $1 per transaction.

A third method is to arrange for a Partial Placement, as discussed previously, where the location owner loads your ATM with their own money. In this case, the location owner earns a higher commission, usually half the surcharge.

The first scenario is the most common and utilized to earn the most money. However, the second and third options require no cash loading investment, minimizing the initial investment costs, and they offer a completely hands off arrangement. Essentially, if loaded by a third-party using their own cash, your ATMs are running passively on autopilot.

How Much to Load and How Often

Determining how much money to load and how often is one of the trickier parts of running an ATM business. Your goal is to ensure the ATM is filled with enough cash to serve any customer who uses it. However, to be efficient, you want to fill with as little money as infrequently as possible. Ultimately, your schedule will depend primarily on the transaction volume of the location and the amount of capital available to use in the machine.

New locations require consideration of three factors to determine the initial loading amount and schedule:

Denomination and Cassette Capacity

Nearly all ATMs are loaded with $20 bills, and cash requests must be in increments of $20. A standard

1,000 note cassette holds $20,000 in $20s; however, to prevent bill jams, it's wise to fill with a maximum of $18,000. You may consider using smaller or larger denominations, such as $5s, $10s or $50s, based on the type of location and demographic, but these scenarios are rare.

Expected Volume

Estimate the expected volume by considering the type of location and foot traffic. For example, expect higher volume at popular nightclubs and hotels and expect lower volume at small bars and tattoo shops.

Withdrawal Average and Maximum Withdrawal Amount

The average withdrawal amount nationwide ranges from $60-$80 per transaction. In almost all situations, the maximum withdrawal amount is $200. If a customer wishes to withdraw more than $200, they must do another transaction and pay an additional surcharge fee. One way to allow withdrawals larger than $200 in a single transaction and earn more income is to charge $3 or 3%, whichever is greater. For example, withdrawing $500 at a 3% rate will result in a total surcharge fee of $15 ($500 * 3%). This tactic does not minimize loading frequency, but it increases your profit significantly.

Here's a simple example that ties it all together:

Your ATM averages 25 transactions per week (100 per month). According to the national average of $60-$80 per withdrawal, the ATM will dispense approximately $8,000 per month or $2,000 per week. Therefore, if planning on loading on a weekly basis, allocating at least $2,000 to that ATM will suffice.

With a new location without transaction or withdrawal history, initially, it's best to overcompensate and load more cash than you think is required. After 30 days of activity, the data will give you an accurate idea of how much cash to fill. If the report shows the total withdrawn was $8,000, then you know $2,000 is the sweet-spot amount to load weekly.

CHAPTER 13

STEP 9 - MANAGEMENT AND DAILY OPERATIONS

Learn Daily Tasks

Operating and growing an ATM business requires performing various daily and ongoing tasks. You may not perform all the tasks every day, but you'll need to find time in your schedule to complete certain recurring tasks on a regular basis.

From an operational standpoint, the most important ongoing tasks are loading your ATMs with cash and paying timely commissions. This requires monitoring cash levels using your processing software, preparing monthly reports, and paying your clients at the end of the billing period. Another ongoing concern is maintenance to the ATMs. If an ATM has a bill jam or if a connection error takes the machine offline, be prepared to visit this site and address the issue as soon as practicable.

An often-overlooked ongoing task is relationship building. It's wise to spend time managing relationships with your customers. Even after selling a location and earning their business, continue to build rapport and trust to fortify your relationship. The idea is to become irreplaceable in their eyes. This can be accomplished by simply by stopping by once a month to deliver their check or exchanging texts. The objective is to make sure all their ATM needs are accommodated.

From a growth standpoint, adding new locations is the lifeblood of the ATM business. Setting up sales and marketing systems from the beginning will allow you to grow at an efficient pace. Whether it's making lead lists, calling and visiting locations, printing flyers, or scoping out portfolios for sale, you must make time for these tasks.

Lastly, with all new locations, contracts need to be prepared, new terminal IDs created, and ATMs programmed and installed.

Setting Up a New Location with a Processor

Once you've secured a new ATM location, the next step is to set up the location with your processor by creating a terminal ID.

To set up a terminal, you need to give the processor information about the location, including the name, address, point of contact, phone number, surcharge fee, commission split (if there is a loader or third-party receiving deposits), and the type of machine.

Ensuring commission splits and bank account information is set up correctly is of the utmost importance. This allows all parties to automatically receive what they're owed directly to their bank account for each transaction. If the split is set up wrongly, money will be transferred to the wrong bank accounts, and chaos will ensue.

For Full Placement, allocate the entire surcharge to be deposited into your account. Then, at the end of the billing period, you will pay commission to the location from the funds accumulated in your account. If you have a loader who will receive $1 per transaction out of a $3 surcharge, design the split so that $2 goes to your account and the loader receives $1 automatically.

You also need to choose whether to have your surcharge profit deposited into your account on a daily or monthly basis. Daily is preferred for cash flow reasons. For vault cash, always set it up on daily deposit.

ATM Monitoring and Vital Metrics

Staying on top of your business requires utilizing the real-time monitoring features of your processor's software. Nearly every processor has a platform giving ATM owners this ability through a web-based portal, smartphone app, or both.

Software allows you to monitor the real-time cash balances, meaning you'll never be in the dark as to how much money is in your ATMs. In fact, most software will create a loading schedule for you based on the history of the volume and cash withdrawal patterns at the location.

You can also monitor real-time ATM health by logging in and reviewing ATM recent alerts. Further, you can program email and/or text message alerts when an ATM is down due to a malfunction or the cash balance falls below a specified level. The alerts will give you the specific error code so you can diagnose the issue prior to fixing the machine.

Lastly, the software gives you access to real-time transaction and profit data, including daily, monthly, and yearly summaries. When looking at these reports, there are a few vital metrics to pay close attention to. The first is transactions per month. This number will help you determine how much money to pay the location owner (based on the commission split). It will also aid your understanding of the location's earning potential. You may decide to raise or lower the surcharge based on this number. The second metric is net profit per month. This number reflects your profit after paying commissions to the location and/or loader.

Paying Merchant Commissions and Monthly Statements

Paying commission to your Placement locations is a routine and ongoing part of the ATM business. Customarily, commissions are paid out monthly or quarterly by mailing a check to an agreed-upon address. However, some locations choose to receive their commission through direct deposit by being included on the split. Choose a specific date of the month by which payment will be received, such as the 15th or the 1st of the month. It's important to maintain a consistent payment schedule to build trust with your clients.

If mailing a check, be sure to include a copy of a statement of the transactions that occurred at the ATM for the given period. This report shows the number of withdrawal transactions and profit earned and allows locations to understand how their income was calculated.

ATM Upkeep and Parts

Regular upkeep of your ATMs is ongoing and is vital to maximize the longevity of the machines. Most new machines are designed to last 7 to 10 years. You may need new parts for compliance upgrades, but otherwise, ATMs generally require only basic maintenance to maximize lifespan.

Basic maintenance includes:

Keeping the ATM clean

- Wipe down the insides and outside to keep the machine looking professional and functioning for as long as possible. It's important to keep all the vital components clean and free from dust or debris.

Dispenser

- Air blow the dispenser sensors. Each time you load, use a can of compressed air to blow dust off the sensors.
- Clean the rollers and belts on a regular basis. Make sure that your belts aren't dirty and aren't unnecessarily wearing down.

Common machine errors include:

- **Bill jams:** When a crinkled or torn bill becomes stuck in the dispenser. This blocks remaining bills from being dispensed. You will need to visit the ATM and physically clear the blockage.

- **Communication errors:** A malfunction with the phone line, local internet, or wireless box. One advantage of wireless boxes is the capability to reboot them remotely, which resolves the majority of communication issues.

- **Replacing the receipt paper:** On average, a roll of receipt paper lasts six months, depending on the transaction volume. Most ATMs offer the option for an electronic receipt, which can help mitigate the need to change receipt rolls frequently. It's a good idea to buy receipt rolls in bulk and store extras inside the locked bottom of the machine.

If you run into a problem that you can't solve on your own, most ATM manufacturers and processors have a 24/7 tech support line that you can call if you need any help.

Parts of an ATM Machine

These are the parts of an ATM to become familiar with:

- **Screen:** Provides an interface for customers to interact with the ATM computer to do a transaction. It's also possible to customize the screen by adding your logo or other images for marketing purposes.

- **Card reader:** Interprets a customer's information from bank cards stored in an EMV chip or magnetic stripe.
- **Pin pad:** Allows the cardholder or programmer to make selections and input information and communicate with the software.
- **Receipt printer:** Prints a physical record of transactions and requires machine-specific receipt paper.
- **Cassette:** Where the bills are inserted and stored for customer withdrawal.
- **Dispenser:** Pushes cash from the cassette to the withdrawal slot through conveyor belts.
- **Vault:** Houses the cassette and dispenser, which hold the cash and push it through to the withdrawal slot when cash is requested.
- **Lock to enter vault:** Electronic six-digit combination or classical dial used to gain access to the vault where the cash is stored.
- **Modem/wireless box:** Provides a phone, internet, or cellular signal to the ATM to communicate with the data terminal.

CHAPTER 14

STEP 10 - SCALING

Advanced: Using Leverage to Add Locations

Scaling your ATM business means growing your revenue by adding more locations and revenue streams. The more locations you have, the more transactions and profit you will make. After properly maintaining your current locations as described in the previous chapter, adding more is your primary goal. If you are profiting $200/month from one location, imagine owning ten locations paying you $200/month, or 20, or even 50. At 50 locations, and earning $200/month from each, your profit is $10,000/month.

The most common method used by businesses to discover additional locations to place or sell ATMs is door-to-door sales. This is done by visiting potential locations in person and speaking to an owner or manager face-to-face about your ATM service. While this method is effective, it's also slow, time-consuming, and linear. If you are the owner and sole employee of your business, it's difficult to visit many locations daily, especially if traveling far from your home. The following are additional methods to stack on top of door-to-door sales and enhance effectiveness:

Physical Marketing

Physical marketing is a classic, time-tested method of attracting potential customers to you rather than seeking them out. Hanging up or handing out flyers and sending out mailers are leveraged techniques of letting businesses know that your services exist. Leverage enables you to reach many business owners who would benefit from your ATM service who you'd otherwise be unable to connect to on foot or through cold calling. By becoming visible to them through your flyer or mailer, they can get in touch with you to discuss their options and set an appointment to meet. Physical marketing also portrays you as a serious business and not merely soliciting. You are someone to take seriously, and your materials will likely be kept or even shared with another business in the form of a referral.

Digital Marketing

In addition to physical marketing campaigns, create digital marketing campaigns. In today's business world, digital marketing is paramount. Digital marketing requires developing an online presence with a website and social media. The first step to begin digital marketing is to create a professional website explaining who you are and detailing the services you offer. Content to add to your site includes blog articles, explainer videos, tips and tricks, or anything else of value to visitors to build their trust and interest. Next, link your website to Google, Facebook, and Instagram to use of their microtargeting services, allowing you to target your ideal customer with ads catered to their needs.

Not only does building an online presence give you an air of legitimacy in the eyes of potential customers, it opens you up to exponentially more customers in comparison to canvasing and physical marketing.

Hire Outside Salespeople

A smart strategy is to hire outside salespeople on a commission-only basis. In theory, you can have an unlimited amount of people searching for locations around your city or any other city. The more lines you have in the water, the more likely it is you will catch a fish. In exchange for signing agreements with locations, you pay them a commission. For example, a salesperson signs an agreement (the agreement you drafted) with a local liquor store for your ATM service. You schedule an installation planned for a week later. Once the ATM is installed and processing transactions, you compensate the salesperson with $500 commission for the signed agreement.

This strategy requires finding skilled, motivated people willing to work independently to acquire sites. From the beginning, it's important you establish clear expectations and a commission structure worth their while. You must be detailed and coach them on exactly what types of locations to go after and offers to propose and accept.

As mentioned above, the brilliant part of this strategy is you can have an unlimited number of people scouring locations for you because they are paid only for results.

Purchase Established ATM Locations or Routes

A quick and effective way to grow your portfolio is to purchase sites from another business or a business dedicated to location wholesaling. With this method, you are looking to purchase contracts and/or ATMs for already-established ATM locations. You simply take over the agreement, processing, management, and profit in exchange for a negotiated amount.

Sites will either be seasoned or unseasoned. Seasoned sites are those with ATMs already operating with a lengthy transaction history and sold by another ATM operator similar to you. Unseasoned sites are new, but a wholesaler is selling the contract only. Wholesalers are in the business of acquiring and selling as many locations as quickly as possible. They have no interest in operating the ATM location at all. Sellers of seasoned sites typically require anywhere from 12-24 months profit as the selling price. Unseasoned sites are usually sold for a flat rate.

To find routes for sale, the best options are to search online for listings on Craigslist, use an ATM route broker, or a business broker. Similar to real estate, brokers work with sellers to find buyers for their ATM locations. Your processor is also a great resource as they are deeply plugged into the ATM route selling market. They can connect you with potential sellers who have not formally listed their businesses.

Important considerations to keep in mind when evaluating locations to purchase include long-term agreements, EMV upgraded ATMs in good condition, low commissions, high margins, and high volume.

Referrals and Word of Mouth

A highly effective technique for acquiring new clients is to incentivize your current satisfied clients to seek out business for you. Current clients are interested in promoting your services to their friends in exchange for a finder's fee or referral bonus. Further, referrers are encouraged to deliver high-quality clients to ensure their reputation remains intact.

An idea to take advantage of referrals is to mail an explanation of your referral bonus structure to each of your clients and follow up with a phone call to ensure they understand their opportunity. Based on their feedback, you may want to adjust your structure to make the incentives strong enough. Follow up periodically to see if they have made any progress. This is also a prime opportunity to fortify and grow your relationships with current clients.

Trade Shows

Attending a trade show as an attendee or as an exhibitor is a great way to gain exposure for your services. Whether the show is centered on convenience stores, nightclubs and restaurants, or hotels, there is an angle for you to make a deal. It's possible to become a master distributor in any of these industries. For example, signing a master distributorship with a hotel can lead to your ATMs being installed in every hotel location of that chain, old and new. Likewise, a gas station owner in your city may want your services in 20 stations. Trade shows are a great way to grow exponentially. The downside is that attending trade shows can be expensive and time-consuming, but the upside might be too abundant to overlook.

Create Standard Operating Procedures and Streamline

Growth in your business is inevitably going to lead to a greater volume of daily, weekly, monthly, and annual tasks that require your attention. Creating standard operating procedures will streamline your tasks, ensuring your business runs efficiently and grows steadily. Here are some strategies to implement to streamline your business:

Standard Placement Deal Agreements

The general importance of using Placement Agreements was emphasized in earlier chapters. However, equally important, is creating a proprietary agreement that's suitable to sign for any location. The time spent drafting this document is worthwhile as you can use it infinite times only making minor adjustments. Further, starting from scratch writing an agreement each time you are working to sign a new location is an inefficient use of you time.

New Location Sheet

Any time you sign an agreement with a new location, you need to communicate pertinent information about the location to your processor for them to generate a new terminal. Generally, to set up the terminal properly, the processor requires the name, type of business, address, contact phone number, model of ATM that will be installed, method of connection, and the surcharge amount. Creating a standard form initially will allow you or a future employee to easily communicate this information to your processor.

Installation and Programming Checklist

If you are handling programming and installations on your own, it's wise to create a checklist to make certain that all procedures are properly followed. The goal is to program and install with the same professional standards each and every time. A seemingly minor programming mistake can lead to the ATM not working properly or at all. Cautiously using a checklist will prevent you from having to return to a location to fix anything that was forgotten or mistaken. Doing it right the first time also builds goodwill with the location. Further, if the ATM is not bolted properly to the floor, there is a risk of it being moved or damaged. Processors have examples of these checklists upon request, and there is information available online to assist. Once you have a degree of experience, examine your checklist and refine it for maximum efficiency.

Sales Systems

Develop a system for acquiring leads of who may be interested in your services, a system for reaching making contact, and tracking those leads through to fruition. Leads are acquired through purchase, marketing, and referrals. You want to make contact with those leads to qualify them as potential customers. Next, reach out to the qualified leads and attempt to acquire their business using your practiced pitches. Record any information gained during your conversations on standard forms you have already created. In the upcoming days and weeks, follow up with those who you haven't closed, and once closed, take in all the information necessary to get them started.

To help streamline your sales and give you confidence when contacting leads, develop scripts outlining your offers and any responses to objections. The more experience you gain with your scripts, the less you will need to rely on them in the future.

Standardizing the sales process will ultimately lead to more customers and fewer headaches. The idea is to create a successful standardized system to pass along and easily teach to a new employee or outside salesperson.

Customer Management System

Create a system for organizing and keeping track of current clients. If you are not savvy with technology, keep a physical folder of all your important documents and notes related to each client. The alternative method is to create digital files on the computer to store customer-related documents. We recommend creating digital files on the computer for efficiency purposes. Further, with digital files, you can create more specific folders within the main folder for deeper organization. The important point is to utilize a file system from the inception of your business.

Bookkeeping and Accounting

From the outside, as a business owner, it's vital to pay close attention to and keep track of all revenue coming in and expenses going out. After all, your profit is the result of incoming revenue minus outgoing expenses. Using a tool such as Quickbooks and syncing it to your bank account will set you up for success. In addition to tracking all your business income, with Quickbooks, you can create profit and loss statements, balance sheets, invoices, and more.

Another option is to employ a bookkeeper on a monthly basis to maintain your books and create financial statements that give you an outlook of the overall financial health of your company.

Lastly, as discussed in the section about taxes, hiring an accountant is strongly recommended to comply with all tax laws and maximize your tax benefits. The idea is to legally pay as small of an amount as possible.

To conclude this section, once you've standardized and streamlined all your processes, business management tasks become easily replicable. This makes your business more efficient, which stimulates faster and more sustainable growth. While there is something to be said about not fixing a working system, it's smart to re-evaluate your standard operating procedures on a regular basis, refining or even changing procedures to simplify or enhance them for effectiveness.

Become Hands Off

For many ATM business owners, the ultimate goal is making as much passive income and becoming as hands off as possible. Once you've built a thriving portfolio, you'll aim to transition yourself away from working in the business to working on the business. Delegating routine daily tasks to others will allow you to focus on the significant overarching tasks required to expand the business and further enjoy the fruits of your labor.

The first and easiest step to removing yourself from day-to-day tasks is to hire a third-party management company to load and maintain your ATMs. Usually, this service is contracted for a percentage of each transaction. Under this setup, you are free from your daily loading responsibilities while simultaneously freeing up all the cash used for loading. Repurpose your freed-up cash to expand your business by purchasing additional locations, ramping up marketing efforts, or hiring a full-time salesperson.

The next step to removing yourself from the day-to-day is to hire a company or employee to handle your installations, maintenance, and repairs.

Lastly, hiring an assistant or office manager to handle incoming calls, scheduling, commission payments, basic bookkeeping, and software tasks will put your business mostly on autopilot.

Increase Your Income: Additional Ways to Make Money with ATMs

If your ATM business is clicking on all cylinders after implementing strategies from previous chapters, you might be wondering how you can leverage your current business into new profit opportunities. Surcharge profit is not the only way to make money from ATMs.

If you have a sales system implemented and on autopilot, consider wholesaling by selling signed contracts to other ATM companies in exchange for 10% to 25% of the surcharge or for a flat fee.

Another option is to become a loader for other ATM businesses by using an employee to load cash from your business. The market rate for loaders is anywhere from $0.70 to $1 per transaction.

Finally, you can piggyback off your ATM relationships by offering bundled credit card processing. You'll receive a commission for every credit or debit card transaction at the terminal in addition to surcharge fees from the ATM.

CHAPTER 15

10-STEP LAUNCH-AND-GROW CHECKLIST SUMMARY

1. **Forming a Company**

   In Chapter 5, we explained why forming a corporation, or limited liability company (LLC), is likely the best solution for your business. A corporate entity offers many benefits, including asset protection, tax advantages, and legitimacy.

2. **Setting up Bank Accounts**

   Next, we talked about setting up corporate bank accounts where your vault cash and profit will be deposited. Some ATM owners keep these accounts separate, while most use one account.

3. Signing up with an ATM Processor

Signing up with a processor is necessary to begin processing transactions. In Chapter 7, we dove into what you need to know as far as choosing a processor that suits your needs. It's best to shop around to find one that offers the best combination of back-office and tech support, customer service, and monitoring software.

4. ATM Locations and Route Building

Choosing your locations wisely and building your route efficiently is paramount.

5. Sales, Deals, and Agreements

In later chapters, we illustrated how to sell your services and close deals. We also covered ATM agreements. More specifically, how to create one, and the importance of having one signed by the location.

6. Purchase an ATM

We walked you through shopping for an ATM that has all the features you need, while also fitting your budget and the aesthetics of the location.

7. Program and Install the ATM

Programming and installing an ATM is fairly simple to learn. In Chapter 11, we outlined the steps in depth; but, remember that you can hire an ATM service provider to complete this step for you.

8. Fill the ATM with Cash

Ensuring your ATMs are always filled with enough cash for customers to withdraw is an art. Monitoring withdrawal patterns will determine how much and how often you need to load.

9. Management and Day-to-Day Operations

In this chapter, we discussed the daily action steps required to ensure your ATM business is running smoothly and with maximum efficiency.

10. Scale

It's time to scale up by adding more locations by streamlining your sales process, hiring sales agents, and purchasing ATM routes. You also learned a variety of ways to leverage your ATM business into new revenue streams. Finally, you learn how to become hands off and earn profit passively.

SECTION 3: ACME'S ROLE AND CONCLUSION

ACME SERVICES

Acme ATM offers a variety of services to help entrepreneurs launch an ATM business. Whether you're just beginning or already own an established ATM business, Acme offers all the tools necessary to ensure your success. We provide coaching, ATMs, processing, custom agreements and forms, programming and installations, parts, supplies, maintenance, loading services, and more. We've truly created a one-stop shop for ATM resources for business owners to take advantage of. Our goal is to make ATMs easy for you.

Alternatively, for location owners looking for an ATM to provide their customers with cash, we can help you with our Full Placement Program by placing an ATM in your business for free. As another option, if you desire to own and manage your own machine, we can sell you a machine, install and program it to our network, and teach you how to operate it on your own.

CONCLUSION

In this book, we covered everything an entrepreneur needs to know to start, run, and grow an ATM business. From learning how ATMs work, figuring out where to place an ATM, to growing and streamlining your company until you are making enough passive income to replace your job, you can use this book to guide you through every step.

Get in touch with us at ATMResidualIncome.com to find out how easy it is launch and grow your business with Acme ATM!

THANK YOU !

Thank You For Reading Our Book!

We really appreciate all of your feedback, and love hearing what you have to say.

We need your input to make the next version of this book and our future books even better.

Please leave us a helpful review on Amazon letting us know what you thought of the book.

Thank you so much!
Sean Fine & Ryan Timberg